Girl Stolen

Classroom Questions

A SCENE BY SCENE TEACHING GUIDE

Amy Farrell

SCENE BY SCENE
ENNISKERRY, IRELAND

Copyright © 2016 by Scene by Scene.

Without limiting the rights under copyright, this book is sold subject to the condition that it shall not, by way of trade or otherwise be lent, resold, hired out, reproduced, stored on or introduced into a retrieval system, or transmitted, in any form or by any means (electronic, mechanical, photocopying, recording or otherwise), or otherwise circulated, without the publisher's prior consent, in any form other than that in which it is published and without a similar condition, including this condition, being imposed on the subsquent publisher.

All rights reserved. No part of this publication may be recorded or transmitted in any form or by any means electronic, mechanical, photocopying, recording or otherwise without the proper consent of the publisher.

The publisher reserves the right to change, without notice, at any time, the specification of this product, whether by change of materials, colours, format, text revision or any other characteristic.

Scene by Scene
11 Millfield, Enniskerry
Wicklow, Ireland.
www.scenebysceneguides.com

Girl, Stolen Classroom Questions by Amy Farrell. —1st ed.
ISBN 978-1-910949-50-4

Contents

Chapter 1 - A Thousand Things Wrong	1
Chapter 2 - Drawing Blood	3
Chapter 3 - Every Reason to Lie	5
Chapter 4 - Who's in Charge Now?	8
Chapter 5 - Here Be Dragons	10
Chapter 6 - In Case the Law Comes Looking	13
Chapter 7 - Turning Secrets into Weapons	15
Chapter 8 - This Might Change Things	17
Chapter 9 - Stealing a Girl	19
Chapter 10 - The Etiquette of Kidnapping	21
Chapter 11 - Hope and Fear	23
Chapter 12 - Running after a Figment	25
Chapter 13 - One Way to Describe Stealing	29
Chapter 14 - Hung for a Sheep	31
Chapter 15 - Might as well be Dead	34
Chapter 16 - You Want Proof, I'll Give You Proof	36
Chapter 17 - Working in the Dark	39
Chapter 18 - Big Words Scare Me	42
Chapter 19 - Nothing But Ifs	44
Chapter 20 - Let's Send Him a Finger	46
Chapter 21 - Intelligent Disobedience	50
Chapter 22 - A Big Mistake	52

Chapter 23 - Time to Act	55
Chapter 24 - Before They Come Back	58
Chapter 25 - The Wind that Creates the Trees	60
Chapter 26 - Coming Closer by the Second	62
Chapter 27 - Face the Facts	64
Chapter 28 - A Quarter-Million Dollars, Two Guns, and a Dead Man	66
Chapter 29 - The Hardest Thing in the World	70
Chapter 30 - Nothing Like a Toy	72
Chapter 31 - Driving Blind	74
Chapter 32 - Just a Friend	77
Further Questions	79

Chapter 1
A Thousand Things Wrong

Summary

Cheyenne is lying on the backseat of her car, waiting for her stepmom to return with her prescription, when someone gets in and starts driving the car.

The thief is surprised to discover her, but instead of stopping, he speeds up. Cheyenne realises she is being kidnapped, but can't see what is going on as she is blind.

Questions

1. What is going on as the story begins?

2. Why did Danielle leave the keys in the ignition?

3. How does Cheyenne know that something is wrong?

4. What does Cheyenne smell?

5. How does Cheyenne react when she realises the car is being stolen?
   How would you feel, in her position?

6. How does the thief react when he spots her?

7. Why doesn't Cheyenne see the guy kidnapping her? How does this add to the story?

Chapter 2
Drawing Blood

Summary

Griffin knows having the girl is a problem for him, but he is afraid to let her go in case she gets the police after him. Instead, he speeds away as quickly as he can.

Griffin had been stealing packages from cars when he spotted the keys in the Escalade.

He drives as fast as he can to stop the girl from jumping out. When he does slow down, she comes at him, clawing him.

He stops the car and wrestles with her, pinning her down.

He apologises, saying he didn't realise she was in the car when he took it. She asks him to let her go. He thinks about it and decides it will be safer to release her somewhere deserted, after dark.

She starts screaming again, until Griffin threatens to shoot her.

Questions

1. What stops Griffin from letting the girl go?
   What does he do instead?
   What would you do, in his position?

2. What was Griffin doing in the parking lot when he stole the car?

3. What does he do with the things he steals?

4. Why does Griffin feel he was entitled to steal the Escalade?

5. Why does Griffin drive fast?

6. What does Cheyenne do when he slows down?

7. How does she injure him?

8. Why doesn't he let her go?

9. What does he decide to do later?

10. How does he make her stop screaming?

11. How would you feel if you were Cheyenne?

12. What would you do next, if you were Griffin?

Chapter 3
Every Reason to Lie

Summary

Griffin tells Cheyenne that he will let her go – later. He makes her lie on the backseat and ties her hands with her shoelaces.

She offers him her ATM card and PIN in exchange for letting her go, but he is not interested.

She tells him not to gag her as she is ill and won't be able to breathe, and he doesn't, once she promises not to scream.

Cheyenne is concerned by how quiet the road they are travelling on is. She is worried that no-one will notice if Griffin kills her.

Questions

1. How does Cheyenne react to the gun being pressed to her temple?
   How would you react, in her position?

2. Why does Griffin want her to be quiet?

3. Griffin says he will let Cheyenne go. Do you believe him? Why/why not?

4. What does Griffin do with Cheyenne's shoelaces?

5. "She did as he asked, but at the same time tensed her wrists and held them as far apart as she dared."
   Why does Cheyenne do this here?

6. Why does Cheyenne roll over to face Griffin?
   Is she clever to do this?

7. How does Cheyenne tell money apart?

8. What does Cheyenne offer Griffin if he lets her go?

9. Why does Cheyenne tell Griffin he can't gag her?

10. Cheyenne thinks that neither of them should believe the other. Is she right to think like this?

11. Why is Cheyenne worried that the road is so quiet?

12. What is the only thing that might save her life, in her opinion?
    Do you agree with her?

Chapter 4
Who's in Charge Now?

Summary

Cheyenne's phone rings and Griffin throws it out the window, for fear their location could be traced.

He is about to smoke, but Cheyenne tells him off, so he doesn't.

She tells him her name, but he refuses to tell her his.

He asks her why she is blind, but she doesn't answer and changes the subject.

She asks where they are going, but he doesn't tell her.

She has a coughing fit and he gets her a cough drop from her purse.

Questions

1. How has Griffin tricked Cheyenne?
   How does this make him feel?

2. Does Griffin believe Cheyenne's "friendly smile"?

3. Why does Griffin throw Cheyenne's mobile phone out the car window?
   Is this a smart move, in your view?

4. How does Cheyenne react to the sound of Griffin's lighter?
   Does she surprise you here?

5. Griffin doesn't tell Cheyenne his name. Why is this the case?

6. From what we have read so far, does Cheyenne sound very ill to you? Support your answer with reference to the story.

7. Griffin gives Cheyenne a cough drop when she asks for one. Does he strike you as a kind character?

8. How old was Griffin when his mom left?
   What is your reaction to this?

9. How do you respond to the image of Cheyenne, wrapped in a blanket, trapped in the car?

Chapter 5
Here Be Dragons

Summary

We learn that Cheyenne was involved in an accident three years ago, where she lost her mother. Her father fell apart after the accident. Cheyenne feels she has to be strong for him and so hides her real feelings.

Danielle, her stepmom, guessed that Cheyenne had pneumonia before they went to the doctor.

Cheyenne tries to concentrate and think. She misses her guide dog, Phantom. She tries to figure out how to use her blindness and her other heightened senses to her advantage. She intends to talk Griffin into freeing her hands, so that she can collect clues and tools and wait for an escape opportunity.

She wakes up to the sensation of driving down a bumpy, gravel road and hears a dog barking.

Griffin speaks to a man who hits him when he sees Cheyenne. This man is Griffin's father.

Questions

1. What details about Cheyenne's life do you learn in this chapter?

2. How was Cheyenne's father affected by the accident?

3. Why does Cheyenne hide her real feelings from her dad?

4. How did Danielle know that Cheyenne has pneumonia? What does this tell you about Danielle?

5. According to the doctor, is Cheyenne very ill?

6. Who is Phantom?

7. What advantages are there to being blind, according to Cheyenne?
   Have you heard about or come across any of these before?

8. How does Cheyenne know what time it is?

9. How does she hope to gain an advantage over her kidnapper?
   Is this a good plan, in your view?

10. "...she wouldn't go quietly."
    What does this mean?
    What does it tell you about Cheyenne's character?

11. What does Cheyenne hear, smell and feel as she wakes up?
    Where is she, do you think?

12. What conclusion does the man jump to when he realises Griffin has a girl on the backseat?
    What does this tell you about these men?

13. Who has Griffin taken her to?
    What is he like?
    Use examples to support the points you make.

14. Is Cheyenne in a lot of danger, in your view?

15. Describe the atmosphere at this point.

16. What interests you in the story so far?

Chapter 6
In Case the Law Comes Looking

Summary

Griffin and his father, Roy, square up to one another, but Griffin stands down. They are joined by Jimbo and TJ, men who work for Roy. These two men go to get Griffin's Honda from the parking lot, in case it is linked to the theft of the Escalade.

Questions

1. Describe Roy, Griffin's dad.

2. Describe Jimbo and TJ, the men who come out of the barn.

3. What job does Roy send Jimbo and TJ to do?
   Is this clever thinking, in your view?

4. "Just give me my cane and let me go right now. I won't tell anyone anything. I promise."
   Would you let her go, in Griffin's position?

5. How does Duke (the dog) react to Cheyenne?

6. What makes Duke the kind of dog Griffin's dad wants?
   What does this tell you about Roy, Griffin's dad?

7. As they walk towards the house, why is Griffin glad that Cheyenne is blind?
   What is your reaction to this?

8. What sort of business is Roy running?

9. Describe the area surrounding Griffin's house.
   Would you like to live there? Explain your view.

Chapter 7
Turning Secrets into Weapons

Summary

Cheyenne gets bumped and bruised as Griffin does a poor job of guiding her around obstacles in the house.

She is glad to have learned Griffin's and Roy's names as she intends to give these details to the police once she escapes.

Although legally blind, Cheyenne has a ten degree slice of vision to her left, which is usually more distracting than helpful.

Griffin takes her to a bedroom and ties her ankle to the bed. He warns her that she is in the middle of nowhere and that the dog will attack her if she goes outside.

Cheyenne mentally files away the dog's name with that of Roy and Griffin and the noise of saws outside.

Griffin brings her a glass of water. When he leaves she searches the room and then decides to break the water glass.

Questions

1. What are Cheyenne's first impressions of the house?

2. Why does Cheyenne wish her hands were free?

3. What useful information has Cheyenne gathered so far? What does she intend to do with this knowledge?

4. The doctors say she suffered a "contracoup injury". What does this mean?

5. What limited sight does Cheyenne still have?

6. Why does Cheyenne often choose to wear dark glasses? What is your response to this?

7. "A bed. The thought made her nervous."
   Why is Cheyenne nervous here?
   Are her fears justified?
   How does her anxiety affect the mood of the story?

8. Griffin ties Cheyenne's ankle to the bed. Do you think this is necessary?

9. What does Cheyenne decide to do to the water glass? Is this a smart move, in your view?

Chapter 8
This Might Change Things

Summary

Roy talks about dumping the Escalade, worried about the trouble they'll be in if they are caught. Griffin wants to sell the car and dump Cheyenne.

Roy stops listening to him, hearing a radio news report that reveals that Cheyenne's father is the president of Nike.

Griffin expects Roy to be furious, but he is not.

Questions

1. "And you could stare as long as you wanted without ever worrying about being caught."
   What is your response to Griffin's thoughts as the chapter begins?

2. Why doesn't Roy want to sell the Escalade?

3. What does Griffin want to do with the car?

4. What do they learn about Cheyenne from the news report on the radio?
   How does Roy react to this news?

Chapter 9
Stealing a Girl

Summary

Cheyenne manages to break the water glass and uses a very sharp piece to start cutting the shoelace binding her wrists.

She is disturbed by Roy and Griffin who come to talk to her after hearing the radio report. Roy demands phone numbers from her, intending to contact her father for a ransom.

Questions

1. Is it easy for Cheyenne to break the water glass?

2. Describe the piece of glass she is left holding.
   What does she do with it?

3. What is Cheyenne able to do, because she was born sighted?

4. What new skills has Cheyenne acquired to help her cope with her blindness?
   What everyday tasks can she complete?
   Are you impressed by her abilities?

5. How do people treat Cheyenne because she is blind?
   What is your response to this?

6. Why do Griffin and Roy come into the bedroom?

7. What is Roy planning to do?
   What is your response to this?

8. Does this development make matters better or worse for Cheyenne?
   Explain your point of view.

Chapter 10
The Etiquette of Kidnapping

Summary

Roy asks Cheyenne for phone numbers so he can contact her family.

She looks very unwell and her cough sounds bad.

Once he has the numbers, he goes to get a mobile that can't be traced, leaving Griffin to watch Cheyenne.

Griffin cuts the shoelace at Cheyenne's wrists so that she can drink some water.

He checks on her often while making lunch, but each time, she has not moved.

Questions

1. Why is Griffin worried that Roy will be angry with him?

2. "She didn't look good."
   Describe the state of Cheyenne's health at this point.
   Are you concerned by how ill she is?

3. Describe Griffin's kitchen.
   Does it tell you anything about Griffin's life?
   Do you feel sorry for him at all?

4. Is Roy a good father, based on what we have read so far?

5. Where does Roy go, once he has the phone numbers?

6. Griffin tells Cheyenne that if she tries anything, he will shoot her.
   How does making these threats make him feel?
   Does this tell you anything about him?

7. Why does Griffin keep checking on Cheyenne?
   Why doesn't she move?

Chapter 11
Hope and Fear

Summary

Cheyenne has lunch with Griffin. Tied to the kitchen table, she eats a hotdog wrapped in bread.

They chat about how her blindness affects her mealtimes. She keeps him talking as she figures the others have left and wants him to relax around her and drop his guard.

She asks to use the bathroom, running the tap to mask any noise she might make. Then she looks for a window and finds one, unlocked. Despite not knowing what awaits outside, Cheyenne opens the window, to escape.

Questions

1. What has Cheyenne learned about the house she's in?

2. What does Griffin make for lunch?
   Does this sound very appetising to you?
   Does this meal tell you anything about Griffin's life?

3. How does Cheyenne's dad help her at mealtimes?

4. How does Cheyenne feel when Griffin laughs as they eat?

5. How do people usually react to Cheyenne in restaurants and movie theatres, once they realise she is blind?

6. Why does Cheyenne bring lunch to school?
   Do you understand her reasons for doing this?

7. Why is Cheyenne chatting to Griffin like this?
   Is this a good strategy, in your view?

8. What excuse does she give Griffin for turning on the tap in the bathroom?
   What is the real reason?
   Is Cheyenne quick-witted, in your opinion?
   Do you think she will manage to escape?

9. Why is Cheyenne good at orientation and figuring out directions?

10. Is she brave to try to escape like this?
    What, do you think, will happen to her if she is caught?

Chapter 12
Running after a Figment

Summary

Griffin paces the hall, calling Cheyenne's name. She has been in the bathroom a long time. He remembers the window and breaks the door open to find that she is nowhere to be seen.

He decides to catch her and bring her back, worried about what Roy will do if he discovers she is missing.

As he is about to follow Cheyenne out the window, he spots her in the bathtub, hiding behind the shower curtain. He hears car engines at this moment as TJ and Jimbo return.

Griffin jumps into the bath, tearing the shower curtain. He shouts at Cheyenne that Roy will make both of their lives hell if he hears that she was trying to escape.

Griffin realises that if Roy frees Cheyenne, she will go straight to the police.

They go back to Griffin's room and he ties her ankle to the bed, but doesn't have time to re-tie her wrists before Jimbo and TJ come into the house.

Jimbo says the parking lot was crawling with police and news reporters. They speculate about the ransom, wondering whether they will get a million dollars.

TJ touches Cheyenne's hair and she jerks away, steadying herself with her hand. The men then see that her hands are untied.

Questions

1. Why doesn't Griffin hover outside the bathroom door?
   What does this tell you about how he views Cheyenne?

2. What does Griffin decide to do, once he realises Cheyenne has escaped?
   What is he really worried about?
   What is your response to this?

3. "He had to hurry and find her before she hurt herself."
   Why is Griffin concerned that he return her unharmed?

4. Does he blame her for running away?
   Does this tell you anything about Griffin?

5. What would you do next, in Griffin's position?

6. What does Griffin see, as he is about to climb out the window?
   What is your reaction to this?

7. What does Griffin hear as he leans out the window?
   What does this mean?

8. What does Griffin shout at Cheyenne?

9. How must Cheyenne be feeling at this point?

10. Why doesn't Griffin re-tie Cheyenne's hands?

11. According to Jimbo, what was the crime scene like when they went to pick up the Honda?
What does this tell you?

12. "No names, dummy."
Why does Jimbo's precaution infuriate Griffin?

13. How does Griffin respond when TJ is disrespectful about Cheyenne's stepmom?
What does this tell you?

14. How does Jimbo discover that Cheyenne is not tied up?
How do you feel about Cheyenne being kept prisoner by these men?
Is she safe with them, in your view?

Chapter 13
One Way to Describe Stealing

Summary

Griffin tells the others that he untied Cheyenne so she could use the bathroom. He says that he has things under control and that they should go and finish work on the Toyota.

They do as he says, although they don't like him telling them what to do.

Griffin explains to Cheyenne about his dad's work with junkers and stolen cars.

She is very tired and asks if she can sleep.

Questions

1. Does Griffin do a good job of covering up about Cheyenne's untied hands?

2. What stops Cheyenne from using the piece of broken glass on the men?

3. How does Griffin get rid of the other two men?

4. What does Griffin tell Cheyenne about his dad's work? Are you surprised that he is so honest?

5. Why do body shops buy parts from Roy's gang, when they know they are stolen?

6. How well are Griffin and Cheyenne getting along? Has anything changed between them since he accidentally kidnapped her?

Chapter 14
Hung for a Sheep

Summary

Griffin reties Cheyenne's ankle while she sleeps and covers her with a quilt.

He remembers his stolen loot in the Honda, but doesn't go to sell it, as he is afraid to leave Cheyenne with Jimbo and TJ.

Griffin cleans up the house while Cheyenne sleeps. They talk when she wakes up and she describes him quite accurately. He describes her as pretty and she changes the subject, asking to watch the news.

Cheyenne's father and stepmom are both in tears on the news. Her father appeals to the kidnappers to let her go, then threatens to come after them himself if they harm her. He speaks directly to Cheyenne, telling her to be strong.

Cheyenne is annoyed that Roy hasn't already made contact with her father. The reporter says that police are following up over a hundred leads and that the race is on to find Cheyenne alive.

Questions

1. What reason does Griffin have for telling Cheyenne so much about his father's business?

2. What is the "strip and run" trick?
   Do you think Cheyenne would be impressed by it?

3. What stops Griffin from going to Portland to sell his loot from the shopping centre?

4. Why does Griffin clean up the kitchen?

5. TJ and Jimbo stop talking whenever Griffin is in earshot. What is going on here, do you think?

6. What does Cheyenne want to do when she wakes up?

7. Why is Griffin glad that Cheyenne can't see him?
   What does this tell you about him?

8. Griffin mentions the "ugly red ribbon of scar" on his neck. How, do you think, could he have got this scar?

9. How does Griffin describe Cheyenne?
   How does she react?

10. What does Griffin do when Cheyenne stumbles on her way to the living room?
    Why does he react like this?

CLASSROOM QUESTIONS • 33

11. What are Griffin's first impressions of Cheyenne's parents?

12. Are her parents coping well with her kidnapping, in your view?

13. What message does Cheyenne's father have for her kidnappers?
    Why does the reporter think there could be a link between her kidnapping and Nike?

14. What message does Cheyenne's dad have for her?

15. How does Cheyenne react to the news report?
    How would you feel, in her position?

16. Do the police have any leads?
    Do you foresee any problems for the police, concentrating on leads from members of the public?

17. "The race is on to find Cheyenne Wilder and to rescue her alive."
    What do these words make you realise?
    How do they add to the atmosphere?

Chapter 15
Might as well be Dead

Summary

Roy, Jimbo and TJ come back. Roy burns Cheyenne's cane and tells Griffin to put her back in the room. He doesn't want her to overhear their conversation.

Cheyenne remembers life after the accident, when she shut down and refused to deal with her blindness. She remembers Danielle, who was one of her nurses at the time, pushing her to become independent and to learn how to live her life.

She remembers attending a residential school where she had to learn how to dress, feed herself and walk without bumping into things. One of the first things she learned there was how to walk with a cane.

Questions

1. What does Roy do to Cheyenne's cane?
   Why does he do this?

2. Why used Cheyenne hate her cane?
   Do you appreciate why she felt this way?

3. Roy doesn't want Cheyenne to hear their conversation. Is this a good or a bad sign? Explain.

4. What was life like for Cheyenne following the accident?
   At first, how did she react to being blind?

5. How did she come to know Danielle?

6. What did Danielle say to motivate and encourage Cheyenne to deal with her blindness?
   Was it good advice, in your view?

7. What skills did Cheyenne learn at the residential school?

8. Describe Cheyenne's cane.
   Why does it fold up?

9. How, exactly, does her cane help her to walk?

10. What dream did Cheyenne have about her mother?
    Does this tell you anything about Cheyenne?

Chapter 16
You Want Proof, I'll Give You Proof

Summary

Roy is angry and worried about the trouble he could be in over the kidnapping. Jimbo and TJ want to stick around, but he sends them home.

Roy says that he lost the numbers he took down, so couldn't call Cheyenne's parents. Griffin suggests letting Cheyenne go and Roy punches him hard in the stomach, winding him and knocking him to the floor.

Roy sends Griffin for Cheyenne and then phones her home. He lets Cheyenne speak for a moment, to prove it is really her. Then he demands five million dollars, threatening that if they don't pay up, they will get her back in pieces.

Roy is aware that the police will be trying to trace the call. He plans to ask them to drop off money the next time he calls, and says that if they do and it's unmarked, he will let Cheyenne go. Neither Cheyenne or Griffin believe him.

Questions

1. What mood is Roy in?
   How does this affect the atmosphere of the story?

2. Why didn't Jimbo and TJ go home?
   How does Roy react to this?

3. Why hasn't Roy called Cheyenne's parents yet?
   What is your response to this?
   How does Roy respond when Griffin suggests letting Cheyenne go?

4. How does Cheyenne react when Griffin wakes her?

5. How does Roy prove he has Cheyenne?
   What threat does he make?
   Is this a smart move, in your opinion?

6. What deal does Roy offer Cheyenne's parents?

7. What is Griffin's reaction to the amount Roy asks for?
   Does this tell you anything about Griffin?

8. Cheyenne says it wasn't her dad that she spoke to.
   Why is this the case?

9. What does Roy plan to do next?
   Does his plan sound well thought out to you?

10. Why doesn't Cheyenne believe that Roy will let her go?

11. What is Griffin's fear as the chapter ends?
What does this mean for Cheyenne?
What is your response to this?

Chapter 17
Working in the Dark

Summary

Cheyenne had hoped Roy would have worked out a trade with her father by now and is feeling low.

Griffin makes some frozen pizza and eats it with her. She talks to him about being blind, explaining why she prefers to talk to people by computer or phone. As she talks to him, Cheyenne feels the piece of glass nestled in her pocket.

Griffin asks about her accident and she tells him the details, something she usually avoids. She tells him how she was walking along a road with her mother and dog when two kids came along racing cars. The one in the wrong lane swerved to avoid an oncoming vehicle and hit them.

Questions

1. How is Cheyenne feeling?
   What makes her feel this way?

2. "I thought I would eat in here with you."
   Why, do you think, does Griffin choose to eat with Cheyenne?

3. How does Cheyenne describe being blind?
   What is your response to this?
   Why, do you think, is she so honest with Griffin?

4. Why does Cheyenne prefer to talk to people by computer or phone rather than in person?

5. What does Cheyenne do while talking to Griffin?
   How is her blindness an advantage here?

6. Do you think Cheyenne would harm Griffin? Explain.

7. Do you think Griffin would harm Cheyenne? Explain.

8. Describe Cheyenne's car accident.

9. Do you think Cheyenne had a good relationship with her mother? Use examples to help support the points that you make.

10. Why does Cheyenne open up to Griffin here?

11. What is your response to hearing about the accident?

12. How is Cheyenne and Griffin's relationship changing?

Chapter 18
Big Words Scare Me

Summary

Griffin can't sleep, lying on his bedroom floor. He checks on Cheyenne, afraid that she is getting worse. She is feverish. Griffin finds some expired antibiotics of his mother's and decides to give them to Cheyenne.

Cheyenne talks about school and Griffin feels stupid in comparison. She tells him she misses reading and talks about her problems reading Braille, something he can identify with.

He is disappointed that she has figured out his real age. She tells him that she knows he is not like the other guys at Roy's.

Questions

1. Why can't Griffin sleep?

2. Does Cheyenne sound worse to you?

3. Why do Griffin and Cheyenne clash heads?

4. What details do you learn about Griffin's mother in this chapter?
   How does this add to your impression of her?

5. What medicine does Griffin find?
   Is it likely to work, in your view?

6. Why doesn't Cheyenne want the antibiotics?

7. What subjects is Cheyenne taking in school?

8. How does Griffin feel when Cheyenne talks about school?
   What does this tell you about his time at school?

9. What problems does Cheyenne have with reading?
   Why does Griffin identify with her here?

10. How does Griffin react when Cheyenne mentions dyslexia?
    What does this tell you about him?

11. Why does Cheyenne tell him that he's not like the other guys there?
    Is she being kind or manipulative? Explain your view.

Chapter 19
Nothing But Ifs

Summary

Cheyenne is worried that the longer she spends in Roy's house, the more likely it is that her captors will kill her, for fear of what she will know about them.

She tries to weigh up how likely they are to commit murder and realises that Griffin is her best hope of survival.

She talks to Griffin, telling him he's not like the others and that she's afraid that they won't let her go. He says that they will, but doesn't sound like he fully believes it himself.

Cheyenne lies awake, running through her options.

Questions

1. Why is Cheyenne worried that her kidnappers might kill her?
   Would you feel the same way, in her position?

2. What view does Cheyenne have of the three older men?

3. What does Cheyenne decide about Griffin?
   Is she right, do you think?

4. How do Cheyenne's teachers, Mr. Waddell and Ms. Crispin, treat her?
   Which of them has the better approach, in your view?

5. "I don't have many choices, either."
   Does Griffin have many choices in your opinion?
   What is stopping him from making his own decisions?

6. According to Cheyenne, what different people will the police investigate in relation to her kidnapping?

7. Do you think it is likely that the men will release Cheyenne alive?

8. What, do you think, will happen next?

Chapter 20
Let's Send Him a Finger

Summary

When Griffin wakes up, Roy is already up, drinking coffee. Roy has smashed their phone, so that Cheyenne cannot use it if she gets free.

Griffin tells Roy about Cheyenne's fever and giving her medicine the night before.

TJ and Jimbo arrive. Jimbo suggests speeding things up with Cheyenne's father by sending him one of her fingers. Roy decides against this as it would suggest that they have killed her already and would draw the police onto them.

Cheyenne's father has offered them a million dollars. Roy proposes keeping half of this himself, as he is the one making the calls and taking risks.

Roy tells the others his ransom plans. Griffin asks if they will let Cheyenne go when it's all over, but Roy is afraid she will talk about them.

Griffin says that they can make the police think the kidnapping was Nike related and let Cheyenne go on their way to the airport. Roy agrees, but Griffin is not convinced that he means it.

Questions

1. What has happened to the phone?
   Why did Roy do this?
   Do you think this was a smart or stupid thing to do?

2. "His dad never talked about his mom anymore."
   What information do you learn about Griffin's parents in this chapter?

3. What suggestion does Jimbo make to "speed things up" with Cheyenne's dad?
   What is your response to this remark?

4. Does Roy think this is a good suggestion?

5. What figure has Cheyenne's father suggested to the men?

6. "You get a cool half million, and we get only half of that" - Jimbo
   Do the group co-operate well together?
   Do you think they will manage to get the ransom?

7. Why does Roy feel entitled to more money than TJ or Jimbo?
   Is this fair, in your opinion?

8. What is Roy's plan?
   Does it sound well thought out to you?
   Do you think it will work?

9. Is Roy planning to let Cheyenne go?

10. How does Griffin try to convince them to let her go? Does it work?

11. Are you worried about Cheyenne, as this chapter ends?

Chapter 21
Intelligent Disobedience

Summary

Griffin brings Cheyenne more medicine when she wakes in the afternoon. He tells her to play along when the men say her kidnapping is linked to Nike.

She asks him to promise that they will let her go.

Cheyenne is keen to keep Griffin thinking that they have things in common. She chats to him about Phantom, her guide dog, and how having him has improved her life.

Questions

1. What instructions does Griffin give Cheyenne for when she is around the other men?
   Is he risking himself to protect her here?
   Why does he treat her this way?

2. "Promise me."
   Why does Cheyenne make Griffin promise that they will let her go?

3. How does Phantom help Cheyenne?
   Why do people react differently to her when she has her guide dog?

4. How has Cheyenne changed since the accident?

5. What was school at Catlin Gabel like before she got Phantom?
   Before reading this novel, did you think that somebody who was blind would worry about these things?

6. How do Cheyenne and Phantom share the work of getting around?

7. What is 'intelligent disobedience'?

Chapter 22
A Big Mistake

Summary

Griffin leaves Cheyenne to go and make lunch. As he prepares the food he realises that TJ has gone into Cheyenne's room. He runs in and punches TJ when he finds him pinning Cheyenne's wrists, trying to get her coat off.

TJ says that she needs to be taught a lesson.

Griffin sends him out and comforts Cheyenne. She notices the scar on his neck and asks about it. He explains that he got burned when his dad was cooking crystal meth in the barn. His mother told the doctor Griffin had an accident with the woodstove. He spent a month in a burns unit due to his injuries. People stop and stare when they see his scars. His mother left because of the drugs when Griffin was in hospital. She has not made any contact with Griffin or Roy since then.

Griffin fears that TJ and Jimbo will rape and kill Cheyenne if Roy tells them to let her go in the wilderness. He decides to help her get away when the others are at the drop, but keeps this decision to himself. He hopes the police don't turn up before then.

Questions

1. Why does Griffin leave Cheyenne alone?

2. What is TJ doing when Griffin returns to the bedroom? What is going on here?

3. How does Griffin react to TJ's actions?

4. "I was just going to teach her a little lesson."
   What would have happened if Griffin hadn't come back in?

5. Are you surprised that Cheyenne lets Griffin comfort her?

6. How does Griffin explain TJ's behaviour?

7. What happened Griffin's throat?
   What is your reaction to this story?

8. How did Griffin's mom explain his injuries in the hospital?
   What made Griffin stick to this story?

9. Describe the extent of Griffin's injuries in the burn unit.

10. Why were the other patients in the burns unit there?
    What is your reaction to their stories?

11. How do people react to Griffin's scars?
    Do you feel sorry for him here?

12. Why did Griffin's mother leave, according to Roy?

13. Does anything about Griffin's mother leaving puzzle you? Explain your point of view.

14. What does Griffin think TJ and Jimbo will do to Cheyenne if Roy tells them to let her go?
Do you agree or disagree with him here?

15. What does Griffin decide to do about Cheyenne? What would you do, in his position?

16. "Was he one of the bad guys?"
Is Griffin a bad guy? Explain your view.

Chapter 23
Time to Act

Summary

It is 2 a.m. and Cheyenne decides to act, feeling that no matter what her father does, these men have no intention of letting her go. She doubts that Griffin would stop them from killing her.

She cuts the cord around her ankle and walks to the living room while Griffin sleeps. She finds a heavy wrench, to knock Griffin unconscious with. She goes back to the bedroom and swings the wrench at Griffin.

Questions

1. How did Cheyenne, Griffin and the three men spend the afternoon and evening?

2. Why has Cheyenne avoided speaking to Griffin?
   What is she planning to do, do you think?

3. Why does Cheyenne think that it doesn't matter whether her father does what the kidnappers ask?

4. What is your response to hearing what TJ whispered in Cheyenne's ear?

5. What is the atmosphere like at this point?

6. What would you do now, if you were Cheyenne?

7. "But saving her from a would-be rapist was one thing." Why does Cheyenne doubt that Griffin would stop the others from killing her?
   Do you understand why she feels this way?

8. "She would have liked to have cut his throat. And she could have done it, too."
   Does Cheyenne surprise you here?

9. How does Cheyenne free her ankle?

10. What weapon does Cheyenne find in the living room? What does she intend to do with it?

11. What does Cheyenne do with the wrench?
What is your reaction to her actions here?

Chapter 24
Before They Come Back

Summary

Cheyenne is in tears after striking Griffin with the wrench. He started yelling after the first blow, so she struck him again and fears she killed him.

She knows she doesn't have much time before the men return, so gets moving. She decides to find a car antenna to use as an emergency cane.

Duke charges at her outside, but is stopped by his chain. Cheyenne approaches him slowly, giving him kibble from her pocket. He doesn't snap at her. Using her belt as a leash, she unchains him and they leave together.

Questions

1. What does Cheyenne do to Griffin?
   Do you feel sorry for Griffin?
   Does he deserve this?
   Could you do this, in Cheyenne's position? Explain your response.

2. What is her reaction to what she has done?
   Does this tell you anything about her?

3. What does Cheyenne decide to use as an emergency cane?

4. How does Cheyenne approach Duke?

5. How does the dog react to her?

6. What does she use as a lead?

7. Are you surprised that Cheyenne takes Duke with her?
   Did you anticipate this development? Explain your answer.

Chapter 25
The Wind that Creates the Trees

Summary

Cheyenne and Duke set off through the woods. It is slow going and extremely cold.

A little after 7 a.m. she hears rustling and Duke begins to bark. Cheyenne realises it is a small animal and loses Duke as he chases after it.

Alone and suffering badly from the cold, Cheyenne fashions a cane from a branch.

It begins to snow, meaning that Cheyenne will soon leave a trail of footprints behind her.

Questions

1. Is Duke much help to Cheyenne?

2. Why is it slow going through the woods for Cheyenne and Duke?

3. What makes Duke bark?

4. How is Cheyenne suffering from the cold?

5. How is her health at his point?

6. Why is the snow a problem for Cheyenne?

Chapter 26
Coming Closer by the Second

Summary

Cheyenne hears someone following her and hides in a bush. Unable to stop herself, Cheyenne coughs and is found by Griffin.

She is surprised he is alive and assumes he has been sent to kill her.

He explains that he had been planning to help her and they get going.

Questions

1. What does Cheyenne hear that makes her panic?

2. Where does she hide?

3. How does her blindness affect her ability to hide?

4. How does she know that the breathing she hears doesn't belong to a rescuer?

5. How does she give away her location?

6. Who has found her?
   Does this surprise you?

7. What does she expect to happen next?
   Is she brave here, in your opinion?

8. Griffin says that Cheyenne can tell the cops that he helped her. Will this change anything in their view, do you think?

9. Why is Griffin helping her?
   Are you surprised by this development?
   Would you help Cheyenne, in Griffin's position?

10. In this chapter, Griffin says anyone can be capable of violence. Do you believe this is true?

Chapter 27
Face the Facts

Summary

Two hours earlier Griffin woke up and discovered his head injury and Cheyenne's disappearance. He searched the house before setting out after her.

As he walks through the woods with Cheyenne, Griffin steps in a burrow and hurts his ankle. He is in tremendous pain and thinks that it is broken. His foot points the wrong way.

Cheyenne tries to pull Griffin clear of the burrow and he topples over in agony. He realises that he cannot walk and tells Cheyenne she will have to go on alone.

Questions

1. Why did Griffin search the house when he woke up?

2. Why is Griffin keen to find Cheyenne before the others do?
   How would you feel, in his position?

3. How does Griffin get injured as he walks through the wood with Cheyenne?
   How does this complicate things for him?

4. Describe the pain in Griffin's ankle.
   Does it sound serious?

5. What happens when Griffin tries to free his foot?

6. What does Griffin's injury mean for Cheyenne?

7. Describe the atmosphere at this point.

8. Is Griffin an especially unlucky character, do you think?

Chapter 28
A Quarter-Million Dollars, Two Guns, and a Dead Man

Summary

Griffin lies shivering on the forest floor. He is in shock and a great deal of pain. He hears Jimbo and TJ approaching, discussing what they will do with their share of the money.

Griffin says he was tracking Cheyenne when he got hurt, but they don't believe him. Jimbo sees Cheyenne's scarf on the ground and thinks that Griffin has killed her.

Jimbo goes on to tell Griffin that his mother is buried in the yard. He says that Roy shoved her one night during an argument and she banged her head. Roy found her dead the next morning.

Jimbo tells TJ that they will leave Griffin where he is and pretend to Roy that they never saw him. Jimbo doesn't expect him to live much longer as he is already blue with cold.

TJ suggests shooting Griffin to put him out of his misery, but Jimbo stops him, wanting his death to appear accidental.

Annoyed at being called stupid, TJ shoots Jimbo, killing him. Griffin assumes that he will be next. TJ opens Jimbo's backpack of money, but is horrified to find it wet with blood. He wipes his hands on the snow and then walks away, leaving Griffin, the money, guns and Jimbo's body, behind.

Questions

1. What are your expectations when you read the title of this chapter?

2. What state is Griffin in as the chapter begins?

3. What are TJ and Jimbo discussing as they approach Griffin?

4. Why doesn't TJ call Roy the moment they discover Griffin?

5. Jimbo spots Cheyenne's scarf. Why is this significant?

6. "I guess the apple doesn't fall far from the tree."
What does Jimbo mean by this remark?
What is going on here?
What is your reaction to this development?

7. How does Griffin respond to the news of his mother's death?
According to Jimbo, how did Janie, Griffin's mother, die?
Does this shock you?
Did you think that Roy was capable of doing something like this?

8. Why does TJ suggest shooting Griffin?
Why does Jimbo stop TJ from shooting him?

9. What does TJ do to Jimbo?
   Why does he do this?
   Was this a stupid thing to do, in your view?

10. How does TJ react to what he has done?

11. What makes TJ drop the money?

12. In your view, why does TJ walk away as the chapter ends?

13. In this chapter it is clear that Roy's gang have received the ransom for Cheyenne. Are you surprised that they managed to get this money?

Chapter 29
The Hardest Thing in the World

Summary

Cheyenne hides behind a tree, convinced that one of the men is after her.

She heard the gunshot and knows she is close to the road as she heard a car engine.

A voice yells for her to freeze and she thinks that the police have found her.

The policeman is surprised to have found her. He leads her to his car. When she gets in she knows that something is not right about the 'cop'. Then she smells chewing tobacco.

Questions

1. Why did Cheyenne hide behind the biggest tree she could find?

2. What words does she hear?
   What does this mean?

3. How does the policeman react when he hears who Cheyenne is?

4. What does Cheyenne tell the cop about Griffin?
   Why does she conceal some of the facts here?

5. What does Cheyenne smell when she gets into the police car?

6. Are there any hints in the cop's actions or words to make you suspect that he isn't a real cop?

Chapter 30
Nothing Like a Toy

Summary

Cheyenne realises that Roy has caught her, having tricked her into believing he was a cop by changing the pitch of his voice.

Cheyenne finds a gun on the seat between them. She points it at Roy, threatening him, but he laughs and grabs it. As he grabs it, Cheyenne shoots.

She orders him out of the car and locks the doors. He tells her to let him in and strikes the window with a rock, ignoring her threats that she will shoot him again.

Questions

1. What does Cheyenne realise has happened?
   Are you surprised that she fell for this?

2. What does she plan to try to do next?

3. What does Cheyenne find on the car seat between them?

4. What happens when Roy grabs at the gun?
   Are you surprised by this?

5. Why does Cheyenne send Roy out of the car?
   Why does he want to get back in?

6. Is this a tense scene, in your opinion?

Chapter 31
Driving Blind

Summary

Cheyenne knows that using the gun in the car is not a good option. Roy keeps smashing at the window, trying to get back in to her. She decides to try to drive away.

To Roy's surprise, she carefully begins to drive off. She hears a mobile phone ringing and uses it to call the police.

She can't tell the dispatcher where she is, but they use the mobile signal to get a rough fix on her location. There are four police cars in the area and by sounding their sirens one at a time, the dispatcher figures out which one is closest to Cheyenne's location.

Roy smashes the window and seizes Cheyenne's throat. She cuts his hand with her piece of broken glass before he takes it from her.

Cheyenne accelerates again, to stop Roy choking her. There is a thump and a scream as the car drives over something.

The police arrive. Cheyenne asks to feel the officer's badge before she believes she has been rescued.

Questions

1. Why does Cheyenne start to cry?

2. "Could she just drive away?"
   Is this a clever or crazy idea? Explain your view.

3. How does Roy react to Cheyenne driving the car?

4. What does Cheyenne hear in the car as she drives off? What will this mean for her?

5. What makes it difficult for the dispatcher to help her when she calls 911?

6. What does the dispatcher do to help her?

7. How do they figure out which car is closest to her? Is this a good strategy?

8. What makes this scene so tense?

9. What does Roy do when he breaks the window?

10. Why does Cheyenne start driving again?

11. What happens to Roy? What is your reaction to this?

12. Why does Cheyenne demand to feel the cop's badge?

13. How do you feel as this chapter ends?

Chapter 32
Just a Friend

Summary

Cheyenne answers the phone at home. Telling her parents it's a friend, she goes to her room. It is Griffin on the line.

He is now staying with his aunt in Chicago. Roy and TJ have been charged by the police.

Duke is living with Cheyenne.

Griffin is signed up to attend a high school for alternative students.

They consider how everything would have been different if Phantom had been in the car with Cheyenne that day.

Before he goes, Griffin asks Cheyenne if he can call her again.

Questions

1. How does Cheyenne react to the voice on the phone?

2. Why has Griffin called?
   Are you glad to hear he survived the ordeal in the woods?

3. Where is Griffin staying now?

4. What injuries did Roy sustain?

5. What have Roy and TJ been charged with?

6. Why did Griffin call Cheyenne from a payphone?

7. What attitude do Danielle and Nick have towards Griffin?
   Do you understand why they feel this way?

8. What has happened Duke?
   Does this surprise you?

9. How well is Griffin getting on, living with his aunt?

10. What is Cheyenne's New Year's resolution?
    What is your reaction to this?

11. "Cheyenne took a deep breath and thought about her answer."
    What was her answer, do you think?

12. Do you like this ending? Explain your view.

Further Questions

1. What different elements of the story combine to make this novel exciting?

2. Who is your favourite character? What do you like or admire about them?

3. Which character do you dislike most? Explain what makes you dislike them.

4. Does this story have a happy ending? (Consider the ending from both Cheyenne and Griffin's viewpoints here.)

5. Was there anything in the story that you would have liked to know more about? Explain your answer, using examples.

6. Did you expect a love story to develop between Griffin and Cheyenne?
   Why/why not?
   Were you disappointed that this didn't happen? Explain.

7. Did reading this novel teach you anything about blindness?

8. Would this story make a good movie?
What actors would you choose to play the lead roles?
Explain your choices.

9. How important are money and wealth in the lives of these characters?
How important is money to the storyline?

10. Would you recommend this novel to a friend?
Why/why not?

11. What was your favourite section of the story?
Why did this part appeal to you?

12. What was the saddest section of the story?
What made it sad and moving?

13. What did you like about this novel?
Give examples in your answer.

14. What did you dislike about this novel?
Give examples in your answer.

15. Does this novel remind you of any other novels or films?
Explain your view.

CLASSROOM QUESTIONS GUIDES

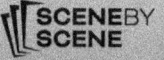

Books of questions, designed to save teachers time and lead to rewarding classroom experiences.

www.SceneBySceneGuides.com

www.ingramcontent.com/pod-product-compliance
Lightning Source LLC
Chambersburg PA
CBHW071025080526
44587CB00015B/2507